Pyrography
The art of woodburning

Pyrography
The art of woodburning

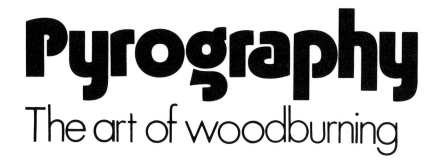

Bernard Havez   Jean-Claude Varlet

Evans

Evans Brothers Limited London

First published in Great Britain 1978 by
Evans Brothers Limited, Montague House,
Russell Square, London, WC1X 5BX.

Original edition first published under
the title *La Pyrogravure* by
Dessain et Tolra, 10 Rue Cassette,
Paris VIe, France.

© Dessain et Tolra 1975

Translation © Evans Brothers Limited, 1977

Translated from the French by Pat Craddock

Set in 9 on 10 point Univers Medium and
Printed in Great Britain by
Cox & Wyman Ltd
London, Fakenham and Reading

ISBN 0 237 44882 3   PRA 5395

Contents

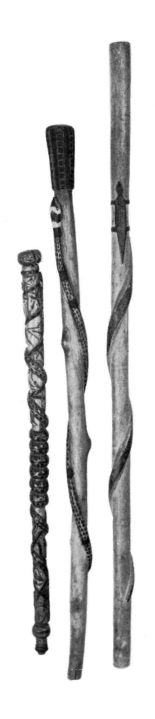

Acknowledgements

The authors and publishers would like to thank the following for their help in the production of this book and in particular the many artists whose work is illustrated.

Museum of Mankind, Paris
The Textile Museum of Lyon
Christian Menard
Alain Bourgeon
Alain Conat
The pupils of C.E.T. of Arbresle
Marc Boniface
Cherubin & Sons, Villeurbanne
Sylvianne Coasse
Francoise Devigne
Pascal Fourel
Maurice Garnier
Jacques Grimaux
Jean-Francois Havez
Elisabeth Ingold
Jean Moiret and Henri Wieczoreck
'La Perolliere' studio of pyrography
Anne Laure and Jerome Robert
Jean-Francois Varlet

Peter Childs and the Leisurecrafts Centre for advice and photographs of their equipment.

Michel Huges and Gilbert Anino, photographers.

Detail of the back of a ladle for olives. Christian
Menard

The history of pyrography

Pyrography is the burning of material, the fascination and magic of fire. It is delight in form and the thrill of graphic expression – to pyrograve is to rediscover a primitive technique. These first pictures show examples of pyrography used as a traditional decorative technique from all over the world.

The method used in Madagascar consists of the whole surface being burned with the aid of an 'aneady', a kind of spade which has been made red-hot in the fire. The artist then cuts out the design and, with the aid of scissors, lifts off a thin layer of burned wood exposing the original colour and making the design stand out in contrast.

1. Pyrograved honey pots from Tulear-Beticky, Madagascar.
Height 26.5 cm Diameter 19.5 cm
Musee de l'Homme, Paris, photo J. Oster   1

2

3

4

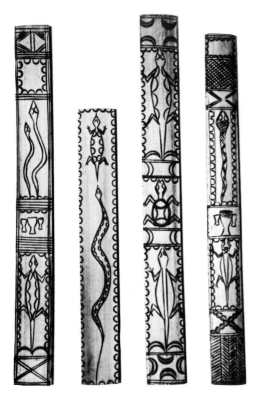

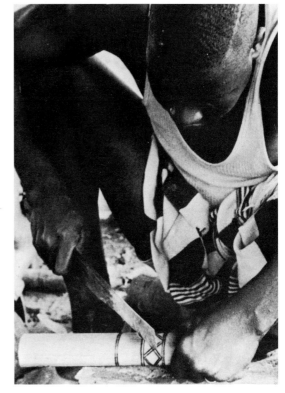

5. Traditional carved 'dolls' for children from the Ivory Coast.
Length 27 to 43 cm long
Musee de l'Homme, Paris, photo Hugo Zemp

6. A blacksmith engraving the back of a piece of palm raffia to make a 'doll'. The tool is a machete which has been made red-hot in the fire.
Musee de l'Homme, Paris, photo Hugo Zemp

2. Ladle in pyrograved Teborak wood used for soups or other liquids by the Touareg people from Agade, Niger.
Musee de l'Homme, Paris, photo Destable

3. Ladle from Algeria, spoon and a calabash ladle from the Ivory Coast.

4. Decorated wooden spoon from Madagascar. The part of the design in relief has been blackened by fire.
Length 25 cm
Musee de l'Homme, photo Destable

In Peru, where pyrography is a popular art, one can see llamas carrying decorated calabashes travelling along the roads which are also used by modern lorries. Here the popular art has not disappeared in a society of today.

The peoples of Africa, Central Europe and South America engraved their eating utensils, their ornaments and their gods. Prehistoric man dug out his canoes by means of fire and wood was cut in the same way in medieval times. Later it became an art as well, Albrecht Dürer pyrograved on wood.

7

8

9

10

11

7. Pyrograved bamboo goblet used for water or beer from India.
Height 24.5 cm Width 7.3 cm
Musee de l'Homme, Paris

8. Pyrograved calabash gourd for lime from the north coast of New Guinea.
Height 31 cm
Musee de l'Homme, Paris, photo Destable

9. Calabash used as a container for henna with a pyrograved decoration. The work of Foulbe women from the Cameroon.
Musee de l'Homme, Paris, photo Destable

10. Pyrograved combs.

11. Calabash with pyrograved decoration from the Cameroon.
Musee de l'Homme, photo Destable

12

13

14

14

15   16

12. Wooden beer jug with a pyrograved decoration from Saaremaa Island, Estonia (USSR)
Height 25 cm Diameter 20.5 cm
Musee de l'Homme, Paris, photo J. Oster

13. Jug of the same type from Estonia.
Musee de l'Homme, Paris, photo J. Oster

14. From left to right: Decorated batons from Japan; Alpine walking sticks.

15. Pyrograved peasant bowl.

16. Pyrograved copy of a medieval reliquary.

In the West pyrography was reduced to a method of marking; branding corks and labelling packing cases. Today, however, the craft has been revived and electric pyrography machines have been developed which are easy to control and use. The traditional Western craft no longer survives but the modern techniques are growing in popularity.

Pyrography is still considered a minor art but it is because of creative limitation or commercial fashion that it has been reduced to a means of copying unoriginal designs and outlines as though for canvas work or wrought iron work. The more traditional uses are not always conducive to creativity although as a means of expression it is as potentially valuable as any other art form.

17. These illustrations show objects which have been found by chance in junk shops, antique shops or markets.

18. Pyrograved calabash.

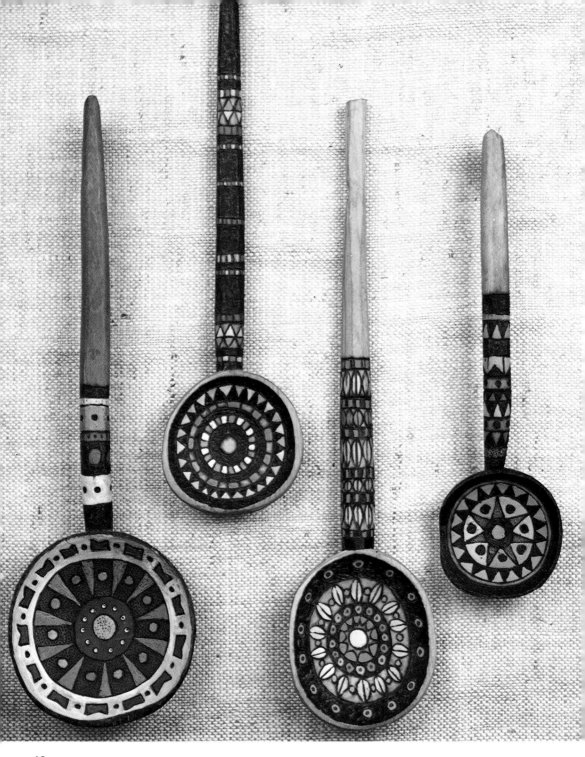

The characteristics of pyrography

The appreciation of pyrography only comes when it is seen in three-dimensions. From a distance it looks like a drawing, from close-up it resembles an engraving, sometimes almost a bas-relief. The light plays delicately amongst the grooves as though on a medallion. The line quality varies according to the wood used. In soft wood it tends to blur and run to create smoky areas. The heat runs in the fibres of the wood and this is a characteristic of pyrography. We use the term *sfumato* for this technique of melting or blurring, in the manner of Leonardo da Vinci. By contrast, the line burnt into hard wood is incisive, clean and exact.

Pyrography leaves little to chance, the line made is nearly always as intended but it requires concentration as the grain of the wood will either help or go against the direction of the tool. By using different burning heads or nibs and by varying the stroke one can produce dots, thin lines, deep grooves, shading and textures. Pyrography can also colour the wood which changes according to the heat used.

It is a fascinating medium for experiment and the examples given in this book will show how the technique has inspired many different approaches.

19. (*Opposite*) Pyrograved and oil-painted spoons. The decorations are bold and simple.

20. Enlarged view of the effects of *sfumato* (smoky strokes) on plywood. Notice that the little lines made with a slightly heated knife nib are without blurs.

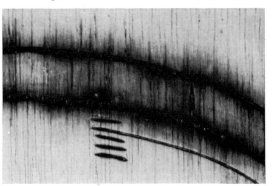

Tools and equipment

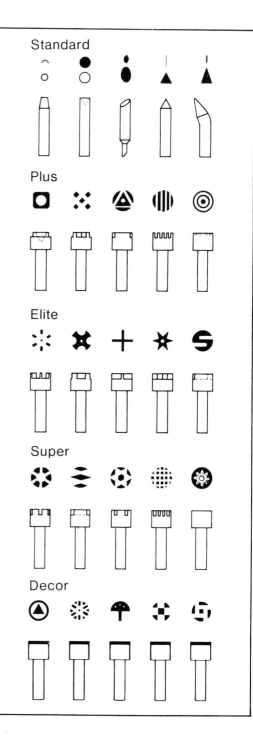

There are two kinds of pyrography machine available at the present time and they differ both in method and use and have their advantages and disadvantages.

Poker type

This tool looks very much like a soldering iron and the different burning heads are interchangeable. The kit is sold with a set of five standard heads, a cleaning brush and instructions. There is no thermostatic control and it is only by turning it on and off at the mains that different temperatures can be achieved.

This means that a beginner needs to experiment to find out what effects are possible at the different temperatures and a certain amount of skill needs to be developed to be able to repeat the effects without trial and error.

The many decorative burning heads which are available are additional to the basic kit and are attractive to the pyrographer who is doubtful about his drawing ability. Another attractive feature is the comparatively low price of the equipment for the beginner.

The diagram shows the variety of decorative burning heads which are available from one supplier.

21. Poker-type of pyrography tool. The illustration also shows the kinds of wooden objects which can be bought for decoration.

Pyrography machine

The development of this more complex machine allows for far greater control over the heat of the tool. It is, however, a more expensive piece of equipment than the one described above. There are two main parts.

The control unit

This plugs into the mains with an on/off switch and a pilot light shows when the machine is on. Precise heat is obtained using the calibrated control knob. The machine runs on low voltage and there is no danger of shock. There is insufficient heat reserve in the point to give a serious burn if touched by accident.

The pencil

This is designed to be held like a drawing pencil and the burning point is formed from a length of chromium alloy wire. One can alter the shape of the nib with a pair of pointed pliers and experiment will result in the pyrographer building up a basic range of shapes for the points.

The kit comes with six spare points and a supply of wire to make your own.

A list of suppliers of tools and wooden articles suitable for pyrography is given on page 125.

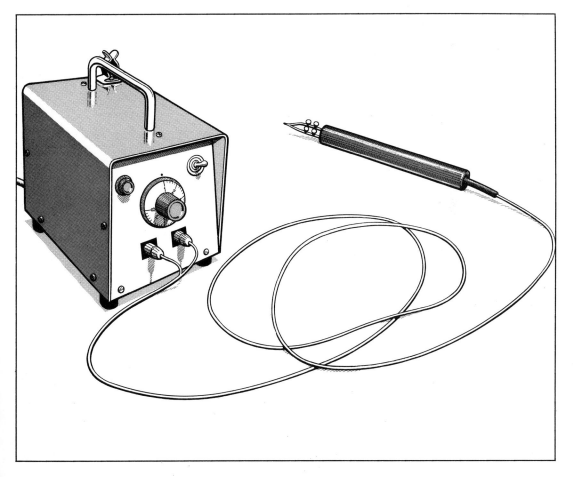

Nibs and burning heads

As already described these fall into two categories. Those which do not automatically suggest a motif, the standard head or nib, and those which are made to give a pre-determined geometric motif. One should try all of them and the final choice for a pyrograph should be determined by the subject, content and graphic possibilities. As an easy way out the beginner is often tempted to choose one of the pre-determined shapes and thus to limit himself to an exercise in automatic stamping. This is merely filling in space and not the creation of design.

As a general rule it is advisable to confine oneself to one or two nibs within a single pyrograph, a variety of nib shapes can look overdone and confusing unless it is well controlled.

Before starting to pyrograph a design, practise on a cork panel or a piece of wood to find out what effects are possible. The illustration of the miner, number 24 is, in fact, an exercise in using various nibs and heads to define the geological strata.

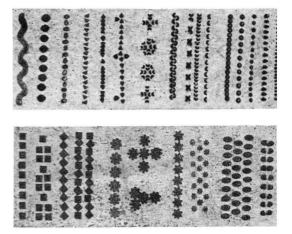

22. Sampler of various burning heads on cork boards.

23. (Below) Various exercises using different nibs.

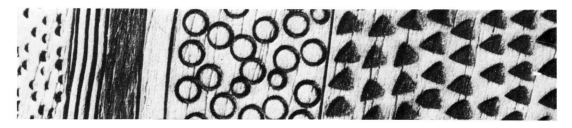

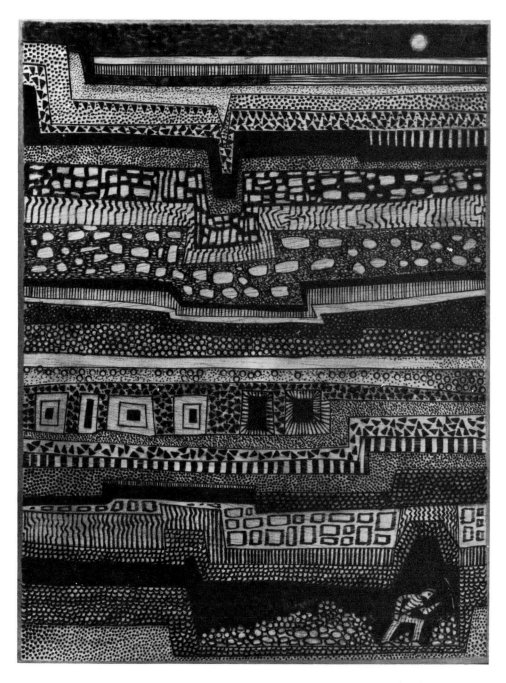

24. Study of a miner underground worked on poplar which is a soft, white wood, easy to work.

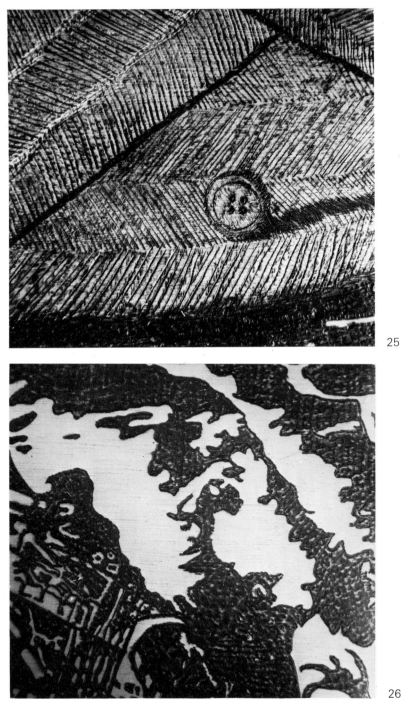

25

26

25. The effect here is similar to an engraving and is achieved using a fine knife-like nib.

26. A flattened nib can enable one to brown the background in quite large areas. Obviously the type of wood used is also important.

27. A pattern built up from dots.

28. An example of using a single nib head, in this case a half-circle, to build up the optical effect of a face.

27

28

29. Enlarged view of a pyrograved board.

30. Details of studies in surface quality to show the range of tones which can be achieved using the flattened hot nib on plywood.

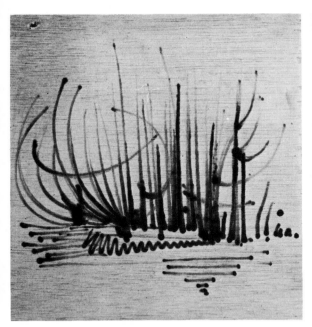

31. These studies show the effect gained using a flattened nib which glides easily over the surface of plywood when it is very hot. The result is a soft, rather blurred, line which is suitable for quick, free-hand sketches.

33

34

32. The bowl of a spoon pyrograved by Christian Menard. Both the thick and thin lines were achieved using a single standard nib and shows the diversity which can be achieved.

33 and 34. Both the bowl and the back of the spoon can be decorated. The motifs are taken from traditional Central European designs.

There is little more to be said about the methods and standard engraving heads. However, it is obvious that anything metal which can be put directly into the fire can be used as a pyrography tool. Knife blades, screwdrivers, bodkins, keys, etc., can all be heated in a fire, gas flame or enamelling oven. Use tweezers to hold them while working. (See also pages 106 and 109.)

A blow-lamp on wood is a quick method of working and hot sand gives shading effects, see pages 76 and 102. Finally, try experimenting with the effects obtained by focusing the sun's rays through a magnifying glass.

Wood surfaces

Originally pyrographers chose a grainless hard wood such as sycamore to give them as plain a background as possible. Other favoured woods were birch, maple, apple and pear. Nowadays the blemishes, knots and grain markings in a variety of woods are used to advantage by the adventurous pyrographer. The surfaces produced by such woods as birch, holly, sycamore and lime are a delight to work on but the beginner might prefer to start on something cheaper such as birch ply or veneered boards. Chipboard, fibreboard and hardboard can also be used.

The following list of woods gives comments on suitability for pyrography and the effects achieved. The choice of wood will, of course, vary according to the purpose of the object, the result desired and the technique employed.

Ash furrowed with erratic veins. It looks white, brown or red and works well with pyrography.

Beech a close grain with a fine, even texture. It varies from off-white to straw yellow and has a tendency to warp. It is difficult to polish and splits a lot at the end of the grain. It gives a precise pyrograph.

Box very hard with a close, even texture. A heavy, pale yellow wood which is sold in small sections and is expensive. Gives pleasing results.

Cherry reddish-grey with brown veins. It is a medium hard wood and is easy to work. It takes polish well but is inclined to warp.

Chestnut a soft, porous wood which is very pleasant to work. It gives a beautiful contrast of tonal values and allows experimentation with *sfumato*.

Cornel (Dogwood) a white and very hard wood.

Holly a very hard and closely-grained wood. It is white to greyish-white and takes polish well.

Hornbeam a hard, white wood which is difficult to work because of the irregular direction of the grain.

Lemon a clear, yellow wood which is very easy to work. It takes a beautiful polish.

Lime a fine-grained wood which is not very durable or strong. It is yellow in colour and is particularly effective for work with dots.

Mahogany a dull, hard wood with a close even texture. It gives a discrete pyrograph without much contrast.

Maple white and furrowed with hard, greyish undulations. It allows precise work in spite of its hardness.

Oak many types according to where they come

from. Difficult to work because of its hardness and veining so choose the softer varieties for pyrography.

Pear fine-grained, whitish-brown wood which is suitable for very precise work. It absorbs stain well but is liable to warp.

Pine a porous, soft wood with well-defined grain. The alternating hard and soft areas could well be an inconvenience but can be turned to advantage to produce an irregular graphic effect. The porous nature of the wood tends to produce a blurring of the burnt lines.

Poplar a greyish-white wood which is very easy to pyrograve.

Sycamore a traditional pyrography material, finely-grained with an even texture. This medium hard wood is milk-white but inclined to darken on exposure. Takes polish well.

Walnut an even textured, fawny-yellow wood. It gives a beautiful polish and will not warp, but it is expensive

Working with children

This is a craft which can quite safely be carried out by children as long as they are supervised. The new machines which control the heat of the pen ensure that the point does not get too hot.

The child on the left is steadying the pen hand while pyrograving the picture. It is important to choose soft woods as a base for children's work.

35. Examples of children's work on plywood boards. Additional shading has been added with pencil and black felt pen.

36. (*Opposite*) The Little Garden. Drawing with a pyrograved outline coloured in with matt oil paint.

35

37

37. Full view and detail of a children's puppet theatre. The decoration has been pyrograved and coloured in with wax crayons. Total height is 2 metres.

38. Underwater Hunters. The pyrography was done on a beech wood base which is a hard wood not very suitable for children.

39. The Bride. Child's pyrograph on a soft wood drawing board. A much more suitable medium for children's work.

40. Off-cuts of wood which have been decorated by children.

38

39

40

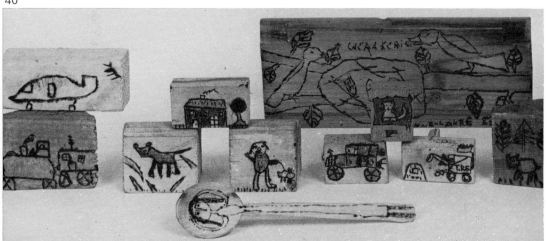

37

Composition and design

Wooden objects for pyrograving can either be bought or made oneself if one has woodworking or turning skills. One must like the basic object and it is worth time taken to think about the way you will decorate it. Hold the object in your hands, study its function and come to an understanding of its form. The design is born from this play between the object and oneself.

By reflecting about the design, whether to use curves, straight lines, thick or thin strokes, etc., the pyrographer comes to discover the problems of composition. One has to consider the composition of the motifs, the balance of one to another, the adaptation of the design to the shape, function, scale and material of the object as well as the actual technique of pyrography. The design must be visually balanced whether the composition is formal or informal.

A formal, geometric design is, in many ways the · easiest to start with. In a circle, for example, the composition can be constructed on the radial lines, the axis, the diameter, etc. These principles are valid for other shapes such as the square, rectangle, triangle, diamond, etc.

For a more thorough study of composition and design see the books listed in the bibliography on page 127.

Stages of work

There are two ways of proceeding. One can first work out the design on paper using whatever medium is preferable, pen, pencil, felt pen or brush. This can then be transferred to the surface to be pyrograved using graphite, chalk or pattern paper. Avoid carbon paper which will dirty the surface and be difficult to remove. Finally the design is finished off ready to pyrograve.

Alternatively one can sketch directly on to the surface using pencil. Avoid using ball-point or felt pens which are indelible.

Finally, when one has the confidence, one can pyrograve directly on to the surface without preliminary drawings. This last method adds spontaneity to the design and promotes creativity and the pleasure of creation.

a

b

41   c   d

41. The illustrations above show the stages of work on a sycamore bowl, diameter 8 cm, by Christian Menard.

a. The plate is divided into concentric circles with deliberately irregular spacing between.

b. The circle in the centre is divided into eight parts, the motif based on radial lines. In the middle circle the design is in four petal-like sections constructed on the axes. A regular and repetitive design is added round the edge.

c. Next the middle area of the design is enriched with symmetrical patterns in the petals with bands to emphasize the contour and to accentuate the radial lines.

d. Final enrichment of the design.

42

43

44

Spoons with bird motifs.

42. The Parrots. The bowl of the spoon has been divided into four by means of diagonals. The geometric disposition of the birds has been made by basing them on a framework of concentric circles and radial lines. There is a clever repetition with inversion of the black pattern to form the beaks and tails.

43. Masked Birds. An apparently symmetrical composition on the vertical axis of the spoon. The whole design fits in with the general contour of the spoon bowl and the shape of the wings. with their outward facing design, plays in opposition to this.

44. These birds are constructed on a network of intersecting lines. The curves are balanced so that the motif adapts to the shape of the spoon and counterbalances the straight lines.

45. The role of decoration can be as simple as that illustrated in Fig. 45 or a complex one where large areas are filled in and enriched.

46. Turkish spoons decorated with a variety of designs. Those on the left have been pierced with a poker.

47. Designs integrated to various shapes and executed with a standard nib.

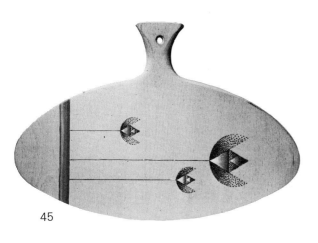

45

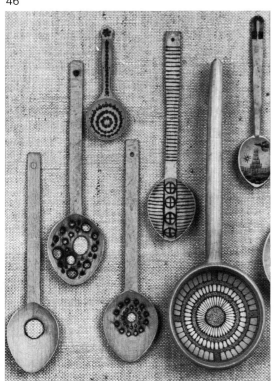

46

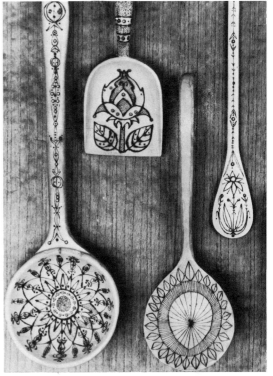

47

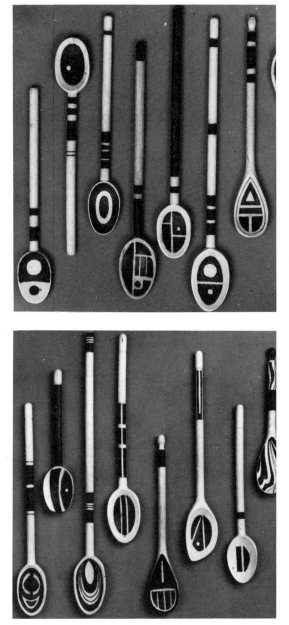

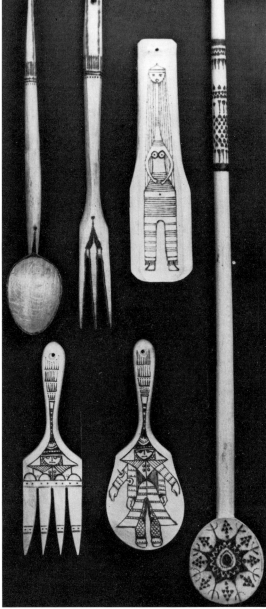

48. These wooden spoons are ideal for experimentation by the beginner. They are not too expensive and their shape can inspire a variety of design ideas. Note that the handles are also pyrograved.

49. Various ideas including a spatula carved from a wide piece of Japanese bamboo and a Yugoslavian long-handled spoon.

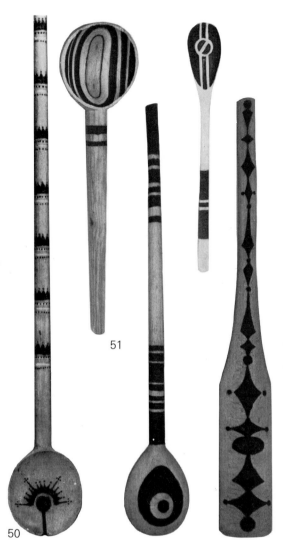

50. This spoon has been pierced by burning right through the bowl.

51. Decorated spoons and spatula.

52. Range of four spoons all decorated in the same manner. Lengths, 25 cm, 27 cm, 33 cm and 39 cm. Christian Menard

53. Boxwood butter pat and a spatula with a turned back handle. Lengths, 24 cm and 20 cm. Christian Menard

54. Pendants made by Christian Menard. These examples show designs which have been dictated by the exterior shape with a maximum enrichment of thick and thin lines.

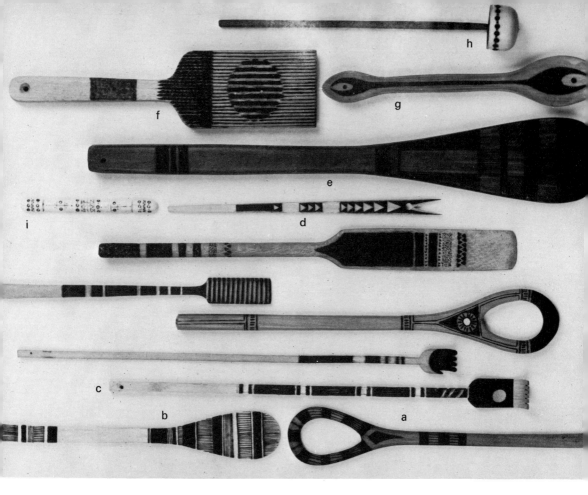

f

h

g

e

i

d

c

b

a

55. An assortment of pyrograved objects from all over the world, including (a) egg beaters from Portugal; (b) flat spatula for mixing sauces; (c) Japanese back scratchers; (d) gherkin fork; (e) large spatula for making jam; (f) grater; (g) double spoon for tasting from Portugal (h) fruit ladle; (i) stick of pyrograved ivory.

Ivory and bone take well to pyrography and produce a precise and fine line when a very hot nib is used.

56. Three birds making up a motif based on an equilateral triangle. The dot technique used gives the illusion of three dimensions.

57. Pierced ladles for olives and capers showing the decoration on the reverse of the bowl.

58. Detail of a pierced, beech ladle for olives showing the interior decoration. Made by Christian Menard.

56

57

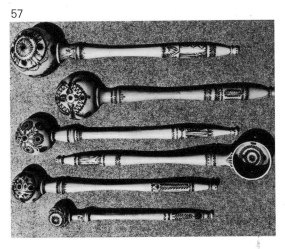

58

48

59. Ideas for decoration on turned wooden eggs. Traditionally these eggs were used for darning socks and they can be bought from a craft shop or perhaps you can get a turner to make some.

These designs are mainly geometric but it is, of course, possible to adapt them to figurative ones and to colour them.

60. Nest of eggs. These have been hollowed out on the lathe and smaller eggs fitted inside. Made by Christian Menard.

60

61

62

61. A selection of pyrograved egg cups. Remember that you can pyrograve the inside as well as the outside.

62. Small objects especially made for pyrography. These can be bought from craft shops or mail order suppliers. See page 125.

64. A collection of salt and pepper pots decorated by Christian Menard.

63. Dried flower holders. These pieces originally came from the legs of old beds and tables. They have been cut, sanded and holes have been drilled to take the stems. Bold patterns have been pyrograved on to them. This idea can be adapted to make holders for other items such as paint brushes, etc.

64 ▼

66

65 ▲   ▼67

65. A selection of napkin holders in various kinds of wood. The one initialled JF was made from olive wood. The ring at bottom right is made from ivory and the beads are pyrograved boxwood.

66. Details of pyrography on small gourds. These decorative gourds can be grown from seed indoors and, dried, they are ideal for engraving.

67. The rounded shapes of the gourds are ideal for small figures. The stalk can be retained.

68 and 71. Ornamental spoons pyrograved and painted with oil colour.

69. Holders for stones used to sharpen scythes. Made from maple and chestnut pyrograved and painted. On the holder on the left the layer of wood round the design has been lifted off with a razor blade.

70. Bread bin and salt box.

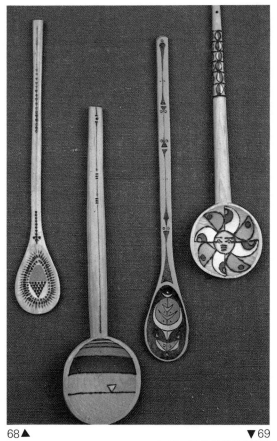

68▲　　　　　　　　　　　　▼69

70▲　　　　　　　　　　　　▼71

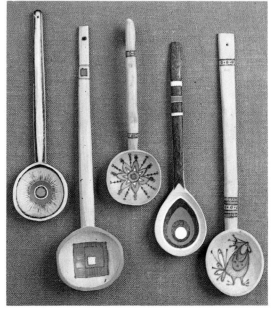

53

72. Pestles and a darning mushroom both pyrograved and painted.

73. Bellows. The decoration has been influenced by
the shape of the object.

74. Antique coffee grinder. You can buy modern
versions in plain pine to pyrograve yourself.

75. From left to right, a butter mould and a goat's
bell.

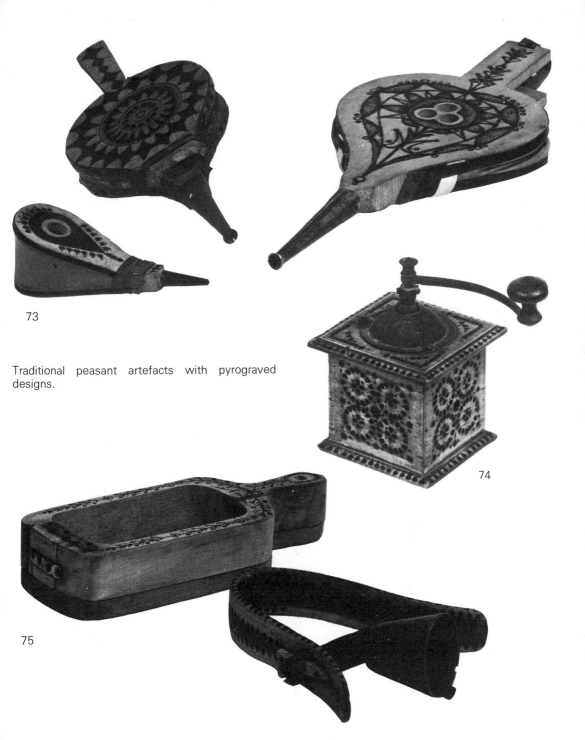

73

Traditional peasant artefacts with pyrograved designs.

74

75

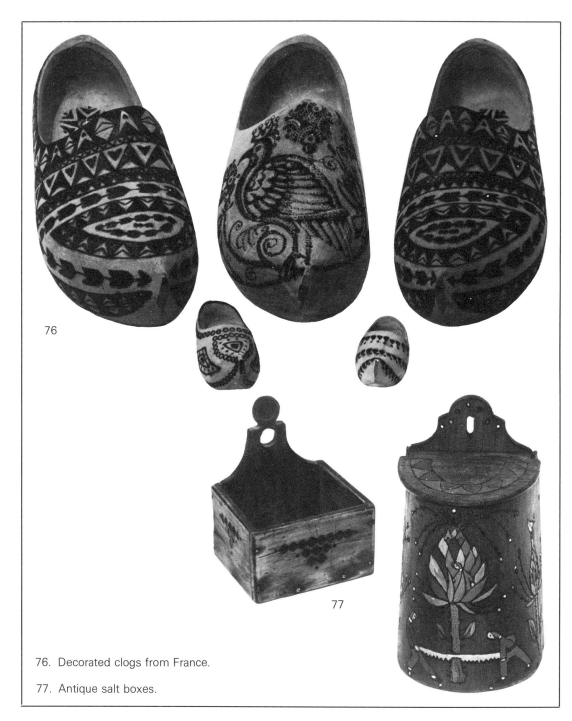

76. Decorated clogs from France.

77. Antique salt boxes.

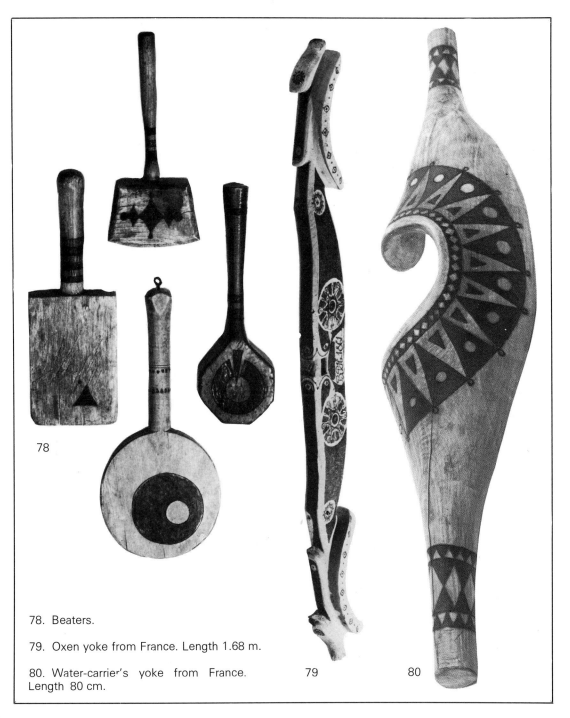

78. Beaters.

79. Oxen yoke from France. Length 1.68 m.

80. Water-carrier's yoke from France. Length 80 cm.

78

79

80

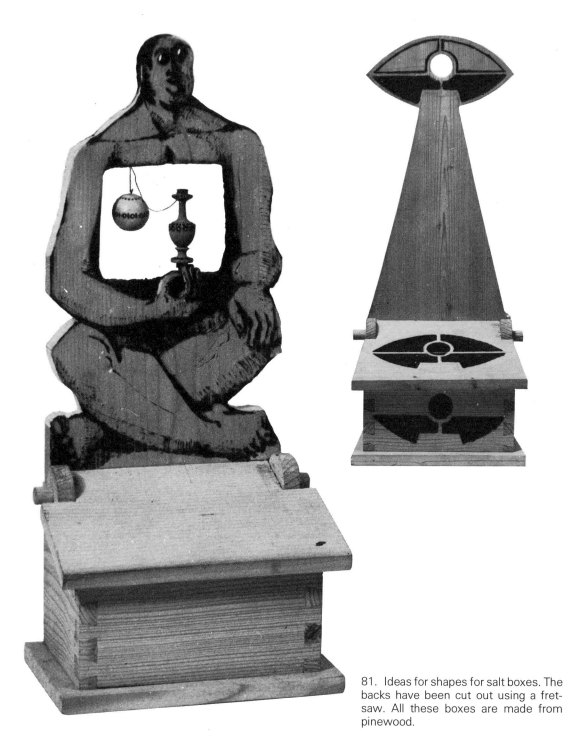

81. Ideas for shapes for salt boxes. The backs have been cut out using a fretsaw. All these boxes are made from pinewood.

58

82. Child's wooden chair with a straw seat. A repetitive motif has been used on the legs and back.

83. Wooden chair from Switzerland. The bold design is dictated by the shape of the chair back and pierced hole. On the seat is a decorated ladle from Italy.

84

86

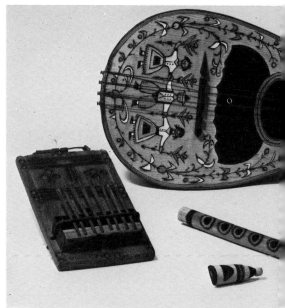

85

87

84. Cut-out compressed cork tile which has been made into a mirror. The decoration is pyrograved with the addition of enamel and oil paint.

85. Wooden, decorated cheese boxes.

86. Leather dice cups; see page 113 for instructions on pyrograving leather. Spinning top and chess men. These latter are made from sawn-up broom handles

in different widths. The board is pyrograved plywood. Many other board games can be made and pyrograved such as draughts, mahjong, etc.

87. African musical instruments including a flute, whistle, mandolin and pan-pipes.

88. Calabashes from the Ivory Coast, pyrograved horns and a decorated boomerang.

88

89

91

90

92

89. Decorated wooden box. Several craft suppliers manufacture boxes of different shapes and sizes for pyrography. See page 125.

90. Comfit bowl, diameter 15 cm, decorated by Christian Menard. The design is based on a circle which has been divided into five. The size of the repeated motif should be taken into account so that at least one if not two or three motifs can be seen in its entirety.

91. Turned bowls and a flat dish.

92. Sawn-off rolling-pin figures. The shields are made from pyrograved cheese box bottoms and the spears are giant matchsticks.

93. A collection of figures made from skittles, candle holders, rolling pins and other turned wood objects. If you wish to turn small objects like these but are unwilling to purchase a full size lathe, there are lathe attachments which fit on to electric drills. These are ideal for turning small items and have the advantage of a variable speed.

93

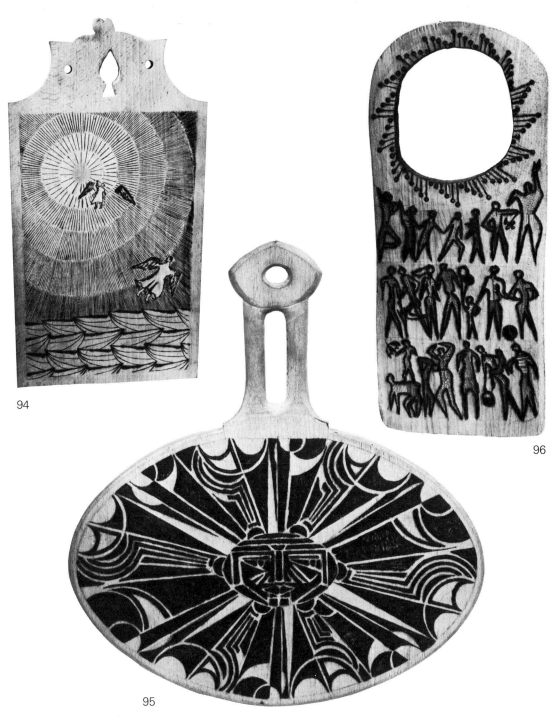

94

95

96

97

94. Fine line work giving an appearance of an etching. This is most easily achieved using a hard wood such as beech. This design is based on the legend of Icarus.

95. The Black Sun. A radiating motif.

96. The Crowd. The irregular grain of this piece of beech adds to its rustic look.

97. Work with a fine knife nib. The design was inspired by a group of children's drawings. Note the different ways of decorating the handles.

98. These two designs show the variety of textures available using a range of commercially made nibs. See page 20.

98

99

101

100

102

99. A simple pyrograved design using standard nibs on a drawing board. The sun has been coloured using gouache.

100. The Port. An effective design depending on the balance of the black and white areas.

101. A symmetrical motif in which the background is filled in with pyrography. The original bird motif was traced on to the board four times.

102. A simple but effective geometric design.

103. A modern pyrograph on an old chopping board.

104. An apparently symmetrical motif inspired by plant forms.

104

103

105. Wooden chopping boards which have been pyrograved and painted. Light beech and dark sipo wood have been used.

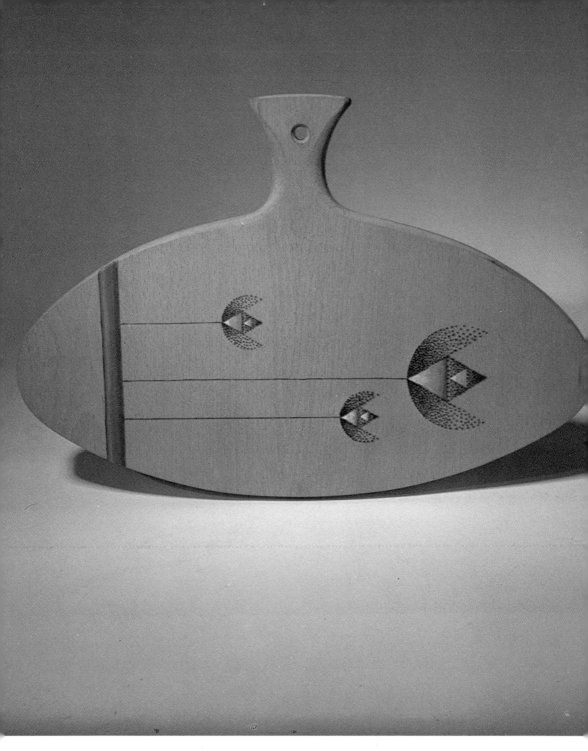

106. (Left). Flowers–birds–flies. A simple but effective design mainly executed in dots on a beech board. The oil paints are used in a gradation of colours in harmony.

107

108

107. A bold design in black and white. The repetitive motif is deliberately unfinished.

108. An abstract design enlivening the surface texture.

The use of colour

The natural colour of the wood is often sufficient for the background of the pyrograph and as the list of woods on pages 32–33 shows there is a wide range of tones depending on the wood used. Sometimes, however, the pyrograph can be enhanced by the use of stains or colours and the following suggestions are given.

Coloured pencils and wax crayons

These are particularly suitable for use with children. They take well on the surface and interesting effects can be created with the grain of the wood.

Stains and dyes

These accentuate the natural shades of the wood without hiding the grain. Depending on the type of wood used they penetrate to a depth of between one and three millimetres. If you wish to contain the dye in one part only on a soft wood it is necessary to restrict its spread with the use of hot wax. A mixture of beeswax and turps is heated in a bain-marie (a sort of double sauce-pan) for this purpose.

At one time these dyes were not very resistant to light and their preparation took a long time. Nowadays one can buy commercially prepared stains and dyes which are easy to use and light resistant.

Chinese inks

Although designed for use on paper these can also be used as colouring agents on wood. They can be diluted with water to obtain a transparent wash effect. They have a tendency to run and are not very light resistant.

Felt pens

These are very suitable for colouring wood in small areas. Care is needed as some of the colours are not very stable. They can also be used with effect on leather, see page 113.

Wax polishes

These can be bought or you can make your own from shredded beeswax in turps. Some commercially available waxes incorporate a dye which colours the wood while waxing. Ask for these at a woodwork suppliers.

Paints

To some extent these conceal the grain markings in the wood but they can be very effective used with pyrography.

Gouache. This does not wear well and is not light resistant. Do not use it on objects which are in constant use. It can be protected with a coat of varnish but the result is often garish. It is preferable to make the paint indelible by mixing it with a colourless acrylic emulsion such as PVA.

Acrylic paint. Applied sparingly to household utensils they can be washed. If applied thickly a relief effect like impasto is achieved. These paints can also be mixed with sand, papier mâché or marble chips to produce different textures.

Oil paints. These are very durable, washable and take well on almost all surfaces. The colours are fixed and have a brilliance if the paint is mixed with linseed oil. They can be diluted with various mediums. Oil paint which has been very diluted with petrol takes on a transparent aspect. Used thickly one can make use of the texture of the brush strokes which are visible. It is not advisable to use oil paint on leather as the oil in the colour leaves a halo round the painted area. It is possible to reduce the oil content by using blotting paper as a palette.

Tempera. This can be bought ready-made or you can make your own by mixing egg yolk with powder colours. The results are very pleasing and look much like oil paints.

Other materials

Enamel paints, spray paints and varnish all take well on wood and give a brilliant effect. They stand up well to washing and use but sometimes they are too glaring for this medium, use them in moderation. It is sometimes interesting to combine pyrography with the traditional technique of gilding. This can be used equally on wood or leather and it is best to consult specialist books on its application. See the bibliography, page 127.

Acids and bleaches

Certain acids such as sulphuric acid can darken light-coloured woods but they need to be used with care. Vandyke crystals will darken oak as will ammonia. For the latter the best way is to place a saucer of ammonia in an air-tight container with the wood until it attains the depth of colour required. Bichromate of potash steeped in water will darken mahogany.

Ordinary household bleach can be used for whitening wood and so can oxalic acid but both of these give a rather poor effect. The following recipes were used by cabinet makers in the past for whitening wood. The ingredients are available commercially.

Note:

Care must be taken using these preparations and it is advisable to use them in a well-ventilated room.

(a)	soda	200g
	hypochloride of lime	75g
	hydrochloric acid	75g
	water	1 litre
(b)	chloride of lime	250g
	soda crystals	30g
	water	1 litre

Finishes and patinas

When the pyrography is finished it is possible to coat it with products which, according to their nature, will protect it with a transparent, matt or brilliant shine film. They will also protect your creations from dust and from yellowing. Most of the commercial products come with their own instructions for use and are available from craft shops or woodwork suppliers.

Olive oil, linseed oil and wax polishes can also be used for finishing. If the utensil is to be used for food it should be treated with cooking oil or olive oil.

To achieve an antique finish or patina there are several methods. There are commercially made products which can give the effect of age or you might like to experiment with various kinds of paint using the brush strokes to accentuate the finish.

Chinese ink, hot beeswax mixed with powder colour or oil colour can be worked into the grain of the wood and then rubbed lightly with glasspaper or scraped lightly with the flat edge of a razor blade.

Hot sand

This method is used by cabinet makers to create shadows on marquetry motifs, see page 120. Fine sand is heated in a metal container and the pieces to be browned are moved horizontally over the surface of the sand held by tweezers. Tone gradation is obtained by varying the duration of contact with the sand. To create curved shadows undulate the surface of the sand with a scraper. The speed and depth of the browning depends on the hardness of the wood and, above all, according to its thickness.

It is also possible to place the sand on to the wood and to move it with a scraper to modify the intensity of the browning. On pine, for example, the hot sand will mainly brown the areas of soft wood. Vigorous brushing with a wire brush in the direction of the grain will bring out the veining.

For an all-over browning effect substitute a blow-lamp for the hot sand. See page 102.

109. Small shovel used for taking bread out of an oven. Height 82 cm. The surface has been treated with coloured ink and walnut stain to give the appearance of age and use. The date was pyrograved together with the simple decoration.

111

110

110. The Madman Asleep. The three-dimensional quality of this pyrograph was achieved by the use of dots.

111. Metamorphosis, the soft phase. Work using a knife nib on limewood. The result is very like an etching. Alain Bourgeon

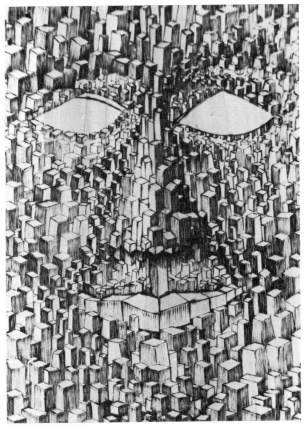

112

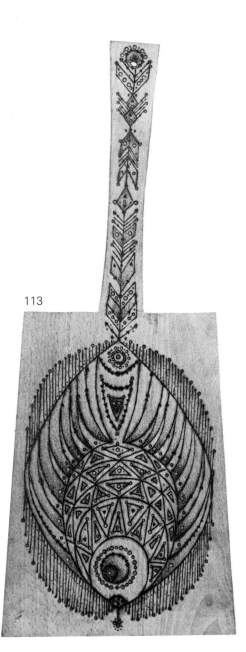

113

112. Sphinx by Alain Bourgeon. An accumulation of shapes making up a face. Worked on lime.

113. Pineapple Fish. The pyrograved lines have blurred in places on this soft wood board.

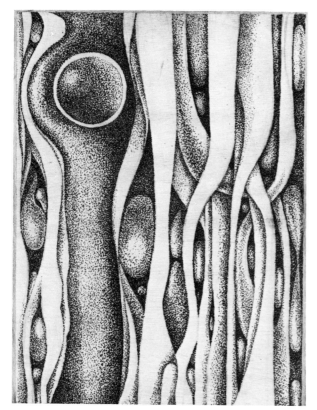

114

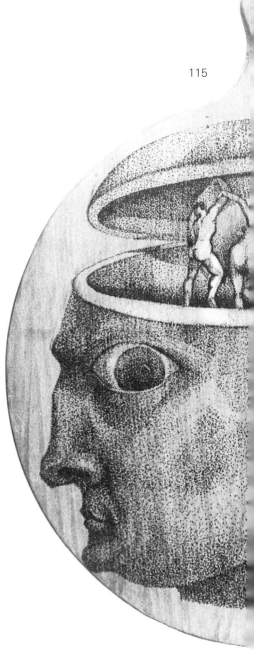

114. Three-dimensional abstract achieving its effect by the use of dots. Worked on a drawing board.

115. Death and the Lovers. A surrealistic design conceived in tones of grey, depending on the concentration and spacing of the dots. The highlights were obtained by scraping. Worked on beech, diameter 58 cm.

116. Using a knife nib on a drawing board.

116

81

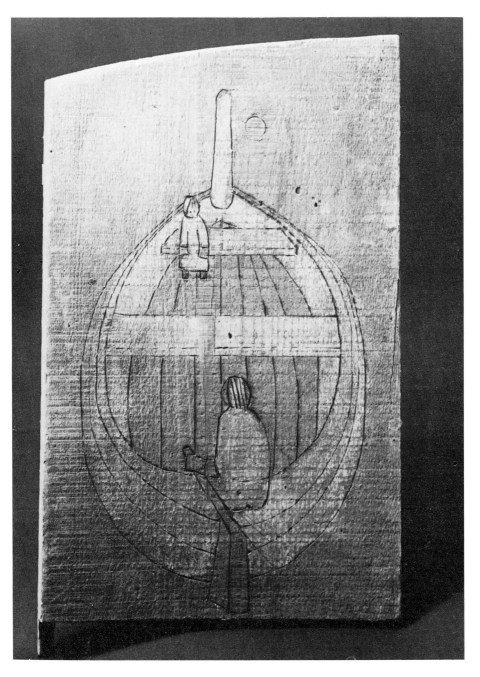

117. Journey to the End of Night. The wood is an un-planed piece of pine and the design is worked with a knife nib. Areas of the design have been scraped with a blade to achieve highlights.

118. Japan. A pyrograved chopping board which
has been in daily use. The design still holds good and the board has achieved an interesting look of age.

119

119. The Town Adrift by Alain Bourgeon. The background effects were achieved using a hot, flattened nib and then the area was stained with red inks. Worked on lime, 20 cm×20 cm.

120. Disintegration of the World by Alain Bourgeon. Worked with a knife nib on a lime panel 30 cm×15 cm. The final pyrography is enhanced with coloured inks, the balloon and crater red and the town green.

121. Voyage in a Balloon. Design built up with clean lines and areas filled in with dots.

120

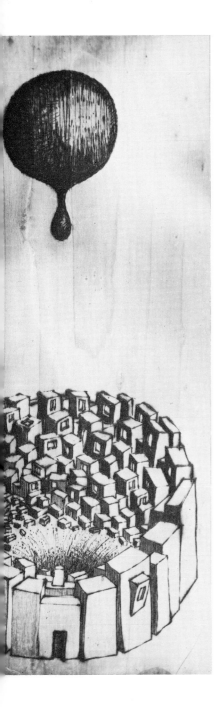

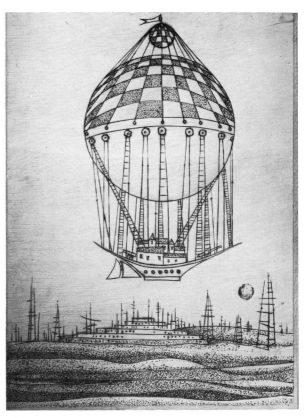

121

122

123

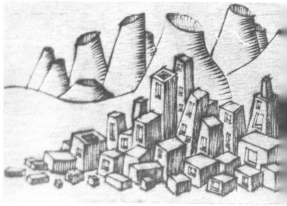

125

122. The Scimitar. An attractive linear design with solid burnt-in areas.

123. Village. Linear design using a knife nib and worked on a drawing board.

124. Poor Wretch. The general shading effects are produced with a flattened, hot nib and the detail pyrograved with a knife nib.

125. Village with Craters by Alain Bourgeon. Design worked with a knife nib on plywood, 8.5 cm×31 cm.

124

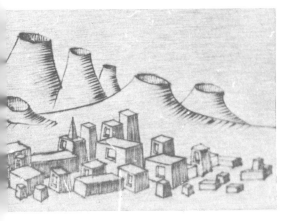

127

126

126. Player with the Moon. A large area of the background has been burnt moving from a solid to a more broken texture.

127. Moon Billiards. Pyrography on an industrial drawing board. The circles were pyrograved using circular tools, see page 20.

128. Motif burnt with three nibs, circle, dot and line.

129. Where does the theatre begin, where does it end? Work which closely resembles an engraving. After the design was pyrograved the whole board was wiped with a mixture of green oil paint diluted in petrol. Further colour was added with coloured inks and work with a felt pen or razor blade obtained the shadows and highlights.

128

129

130. (*Opposite*). The Cats. A cut-out wall plaque with some pierced work. Care must be taken with the design to avoid shapes which are too narrow or thin and liable to break off. You must also take into account the direction of the grain of the wood and forsee its weak points.

The cats have been coloured with a walnut stain and a commercially-produced orange dye. The wood used is beech, 35 cm high.

131. Panel showing a repertoire of motifs by Christian Menard

132. Bonnefis. Worked in an etched type of line on beech. This is a hard wood with a dense grain. The shading of the design follows the grain of the wood. The interior of the board has been gouged out.

133

133. Study taken from a photograph. The design was enlarged using a pantograph and projected on to the plywood. Care was taken over the tone values and glasspaper was used to achieve the gradations of shadow. This technique is very suitable for surrealistic ideas.

134. With experience one can build up a wide repertoire of motifs. A sampler board like this can be used to develop ideas.

Cut-out background shapes

To make a more interesting background to your pyrograph you might like to shape the board or base you are using. There are various methods of doing this according to the material you are working on.

Wood

To cut shapes around or in wood you will need a fret-saw or coping-saw. The former is best used on thin wood while the latter can cut up to 12mm thick. They should be used with a V-shaped cutting board which gives the work support over a wider area (see the diagram opposite).

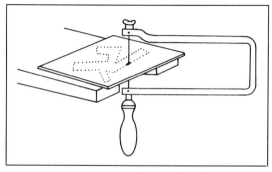

135

Leather

This should be cut using a craft knife or a pair of leather shears, depending on the thickness of the material.

Polystyrene and cork

A hot wire cutter, available commercially, is ideal for cutting polystyrene and it can also be used for very thin wood veneers, and cork. The latter can also be cut with a craft knife.

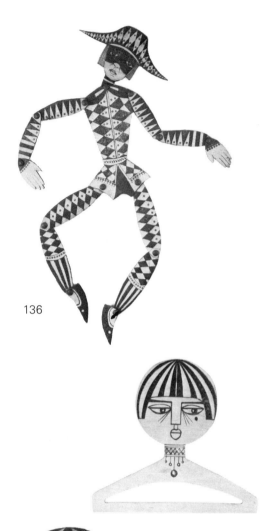

136

137

138

136. Harlequin. Cut from thin plywood using a fret-saw. This puppet is jointed and is 90 cm high.

137. Fun clothes hangers. Cut from plywood with a fret-saw.

138. The Lion. The cut-out shape and the clever use of the line work give this a three-dimensional effect.

139 and 141. Marianne and The Soldiers. Decorative wall plaques cut from thin wood using a coping-saw.

140. Foolishness, Idiocy and Violence. The design depends on the shaped background for its success.

142. Me and Me. A study in positive and negative. The figures at the top have been roughly carved.

140

141

142

143▲

145

146

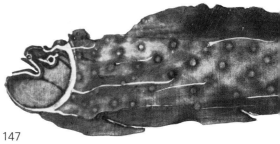

147

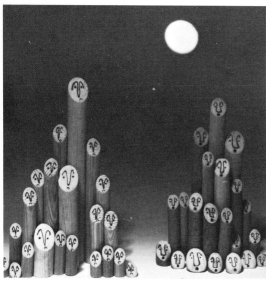

▼144

148

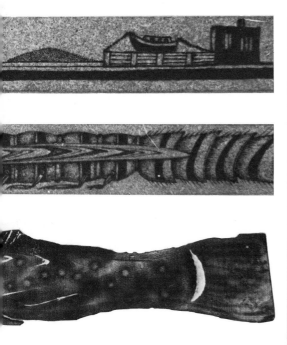

149

143. The Labyrinth. The deeply engraved areas were coated with a thin solution of plaster of Paris and the raised areas were pyrograved.

144. The choir of old friends. Old broom handles cut to an angle of 45° using a mitre box and the faces pyrograved.

145 and 146. The Barge and The Fish Insect. These two pyrographs were made on chipboard which is a good surface for pyrography.

147. The Smoked Salmon by Maurice Garnier. The shape of this piece of driftwood inspired the pyrography.

148. Driftwood circus horse, viewed from both sides. Height 26 cm.

149. Fallen branches of trees decorated to resemble deer. Height 40 cm.

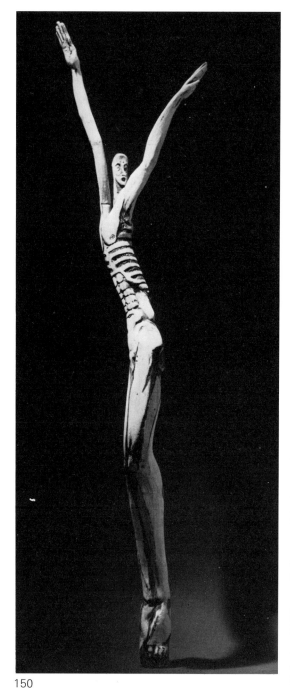

151

150. Dancer. A piece of driftwood which has been smoothed with a rasp and pyrograved. Height 88 cm.

151. The Wooden Men. Twigs vary their angle of growth from the main branch according to the species of tree. Turned the other way the arms would be pointing downwards.

Here is the possibility for pyrography on a grand scale, garden totems decorated with blow-lamp pyrography.

152. The natural growths and defects in wood can be used to advantage in pyrography. Here the wood has been attacked by tunnelling insects.

153. Masks. A collage making use of remnants of wood stuck together. The decoration is a combination of a blow-lamp, branding with metal shapes and pyrograving with a nib.

150

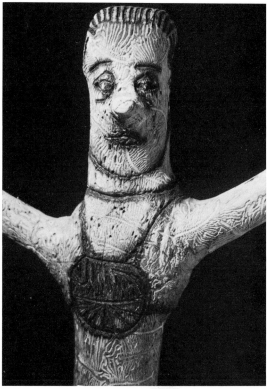

152

153

Pyrography with a blow-lamp

Note: care must be taken using this equipment and it is advisable to work in a workshop or even out of doors.

The blow-lamp gives a fast, wide pyrograph which allows one to cover a large surface. There are two types available, the industrial oxy-acetylene lamp and the less powerful calor gas lamp. Some models have interchangeable nozzles so that one can draw with single or double lines or make circles, see Fig. 155.

One can mask off areas using metallic shapes but it is important to use metal which will resist successively increasing temperatures and will lie flat on the work surface. After the background has been burned the shapes are removed to reveal a negative motif.

154

154. The background of this piece has developed cracks and grooves after prolonged burning with a blow-lamp. The pattern was preserved by the use of metal masks.

155. Study using a blow-lamp with a wide, cylindrical nozzle.

157. Prolonged burning with a blow-lamp with a metal disc serving as a mask for the moon. The plant shapes were added afterwards using a carving gouge.

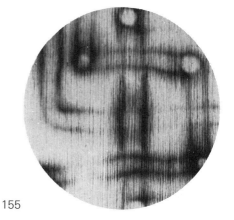
155

102

156. Collage of small metal objects – hooks, rings, etc., – which have been added to a background burnt with a blow-lamp. It is important to brush away the loose residue of burnt wood before starting the collage.

156

157

158

158. Sun. Design made by an oxy-acetylene blow-lamp with the finest nozzle. If the *sfumato* effect round the lines becomes too pronounced a cleaner line can be obtained by planing the surface. Avoid using glasspaper which quickly becomes dirty with the carbon.

159

159. Working directly on to the wood with a blow-lamp without the use of masks. A fine nozzle was used. Height of the board is 38 cm.

160

It can be fun to experiment with a magnifying glass to direct the sun's rays on to the wood.

160. Soldier's stick from the First World War pyrograved using a magnifying glass. The detail shows the pattern.

161. This design was carried out using this method on an old board. The technique needs a steady hand and a lot of patience.

161

Home-made tools

The experienced pyrographer will soon want to experiment and to develop a greater range of tools than those available commercially. It is possible to make these tools oneself if one has access to metalworking equipment. The handles are made from iron rods and the heads are soldered to them. These heads and punches can be used on both wood and leather. Irons can be geometric but they can also be made in the shapes of birds, fish, figures, etc., see Fig. 169, page 109.

Look around your home and workshop for other items which could be used to make an interesting burning head. Screwdrivers, keys, screw and nail heads which have been filed to shape, can all be used.

The heads are heated in a gas flame, wood embers or with a blow-lamp and should be held with tongs or tweezers.

162. Old chopping board branded with a variety of home-made tool shapes.

163. A propane torch made the burnt circle and the wood either side of it was bleached with household bleach. Oil paint was used for the coloured circles and the natural shade of the wood is left between them.

164. Villages (*above* and *below*). The outlines are pyrograved and the colours are a combination of gouache and acrylic paints.

163

164

165

165. The Wave. Design carried out in oil paint which is diluted with turpentine on a varnished background. The outlines of the picture have been pyrograved. Francoise Devigne.

166. The King and the Ogre. Masks made from off-cuts which contrast the natural colour of the woods with the effect of pyrography. Height 90 cm.

166

167

167. Design of circles using specially made circular burning heads.

168. Old board decorated with home-made shapes such as those illustrated below.

169. Note the variety of shapes one can develop when making ones own tools.

168

169

Other materials for pyrography

Cork

Bottle corks, cork tiles and bricks of composition cork all provide a soft material which is very easy to pyrograve using the tools mentioned in this book. Cork can be cut with a craft knife or a polystyrene hot wire cutter and it is easy to stick together. In its natural state cork comes in many different colours, pink, grey, white, beige and brown. It is also possible to dye or paint it.

170 ▼   171 ▶

172

170. A selection of bought cork items which have been pyrograved.

171. Two figures made up from bottle corks and cork bricks which have been cut and glued and decorated with pyrography.

172. Food pot in *Tarro* cork from Portugal used by the peasants to keep their food at the right temperature. Diameter 25 cm.

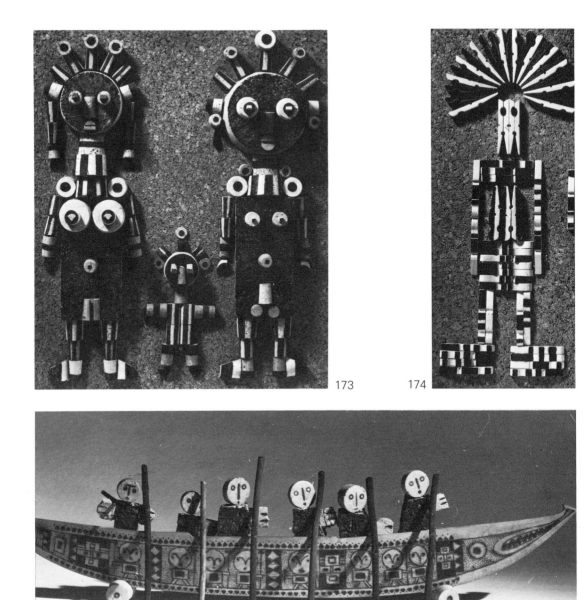

173. Bottle corks, pyrograved and glued to a cork tile background.

174. Collage of pyrograved wooden clothes pegs which have been glued to a composition cork background.

175. Eskimo hunters. This model has been built up from sheets of cork, pieces of bottle corks and sticks of charcoal. The decoration is pyrograved. Length 30 cm.

173

174

175

Leather

This is an excellent material for pyrography and the nibs and iron shapes mentioned on pages 20–24 can be used to decorate it. The nibs must be impressed deeply and the imprint leaves a beautiful patina. It does not, however, resist manipulation and after brisk brushing to remove the burnt crust the grooves can be coloured. Spread a thin coat of vinyl paint over the leather and then remove the paint from the raised areas with a duster.

Leather can be bought already dyed or else it can be coloured with felt markers. There are commercially made leather dyes and waxes which can be bought and used. It can also be gilded but a specialist book should be consulted for this technique.

176. A belt stamped with iron shapes and another which has been pyrograved with a nib.

177. A selection of pyrograved leather articles, a Turkish slipper, satchel for cartridges and hair slides.

176

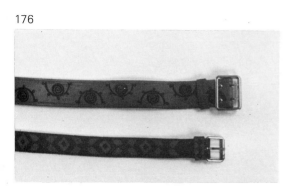

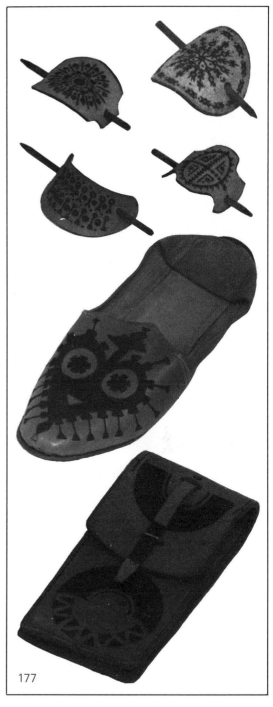

177

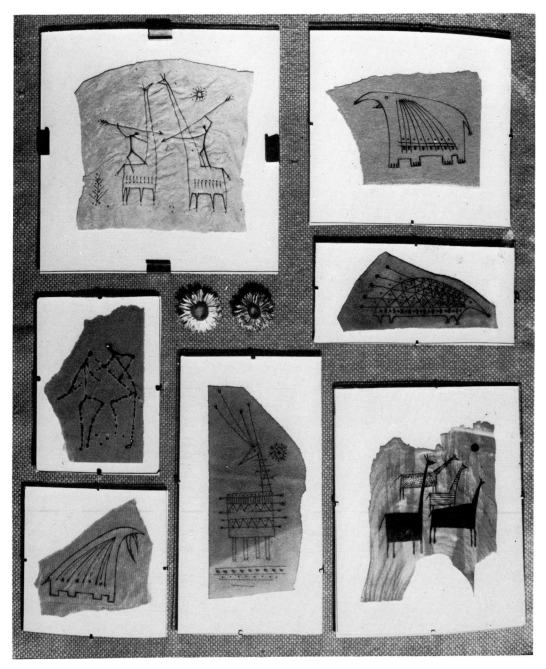

178. Pyrography on many media. From left to right and top to bottom:

Combatants on giraffes — chamois leather
Elephant — cardboard
Dancers — emery cloth burnt with a magnifying glass.
Hedgehog — leather
Walrus — paper
Goat — suede
Gazelles and giraffes — thin leaf of veneer

179. Bas-relief doll which has been pyrograved.

180. Compressed cardboard packaging for bottles made these pyrograved figures.

Papier mâché

This can also be pyrograved and the effect is shown in these illustrations.

179

180

183. (*Opposite*) Pyrograved belts coloured with leather dyes and felt pens.

Velvet

Many processes are used industrially to decorate velvet and it is possible to devise simplified applications for the home craftsman. Some machines have a nib specially made for the purpose but any of the nibs can be used as long as the heat is kept low. The fragile appearance of velvet is misleading as it adequately resists heat although synthetic velvets burn more rapidly than the traditional material.

The effect is of bas-relief and relies on the effect of light playing on the decoration. The shadows depend on the depth of the burning and gradations are obtained by holding the nib in an inclined position. When one presses hard the pile becomes reddened, see Fig. 184. To flatten the pile without burning put a piece of tracing paper between the nib and the velvet. The highlights in Fig. 185 were obtained in this way.

The colour made by pyrograving velvet is not always predictable, on paler velvets the line is dark and vice versa. It is also possible to paint velvet using oil paints and you might like to try the effect of fabric dyes.

181

181. Pyrograved velvet cushion.

182. Detail of velvet pyrography showing the textures which are achieved.

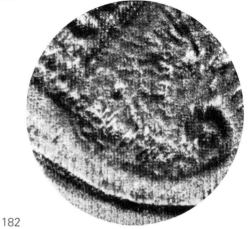

182

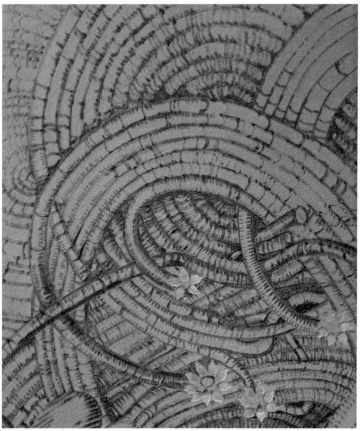

184

184. On paler velvets the line of pyrography is dark but the colour is not always predictable.

185. The highlight on the bird's neck is produced by crushing the velvet pile hard with a slightly heated nib.

185

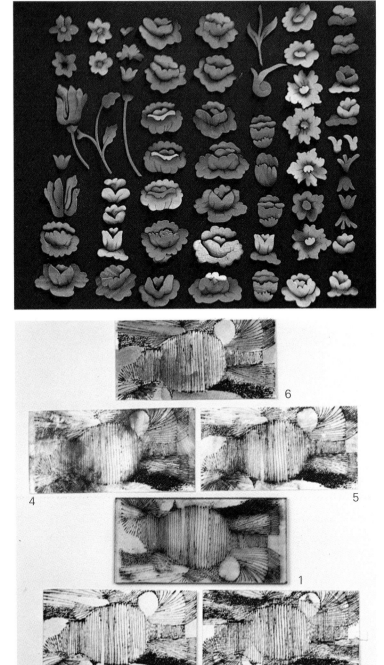

186. Decorative elements for marquetry. The shading is obtained using hot sand and coloured wood stains.

187. Printing from a pyrograved acrylic plastic sheet.
1. Original plate after inking.
2. First pull from press.
3. Two superimposed prints, one reversed.
4. Print with inadequately wiped off oil paint.
5. Print using oily typographic ink.
6. Print using gravure ink, heightened with water colour.

186

187

Printing from pyrographs

a

This is a very similar technique to that of wood-cuts and similar woods, pear and box, are the most suitable. You can also print from a pyro-graved Perspex sheet.

To print as a lino cut spread the printing ink over the pyrograved surface using a roller. Take a print by placing a sheet of paper on to the inked board and rubbing with the back of a spoon. The pyro-graph will print as a negative, image see Fig. 188b.

To print as an etching you will need a press. The ink must be heated so that it runs into the grooves and the raised surface wiped with a muslin cloth. Print on a press using damp paper and the image will appear as positive, see Fig. 188c.

It is important the paper is supple to take the detail clearly. Immerse it in water and then dry it between two pieces of blotting paper. After the print has been taken, put it between two pieces of card to avoid curling and let it dry for two or three days.

b

188. *Top*: original pyrograph.
  Centre: negative 'lino-type' print.
  Bottom: positive 'etching' print.

c

Erasing and re-touching pyrographs

Pyrography is such a definite craft technique it is difficult to correct or re-touch a faulty design. However, here are some suggestions which can be tried.

The whole design can, of course, be erased completely with glasspaper. This can also be used to give tone variations to a burned background, see Fig. 133. You can remove the *sfumato* effect around lines by rubbing very lightly with glasspaper.

Domestic bleach will remove the brown colour of burned wood, but not perfectly, and the grooves will, of course, remain.

A razor blade or the edge of a piece of glass can be used to scrape the pyrograph and will remove errors if they are not deeply engraved into the wood.

As a last resort, if the thickness of the wood will allow it, plane the whole surface and start again!

If it is not possible to remove the fault give some thought to the possibility of retouching the design to hide the error. Simply by filling in an area with solid burning can be a solution. Re-touching with paint or the addition of collage can disguise a fault or draw attention to another part of the design.

This book offers only ideas and suggestions, not models to copy. It is an invitation to a creative journey and we hope you will find inspiration and the wish to create with fire, wood, shapes and colours.

Suppliers

In most cases suppliers will send you their catalogue and current price list.

Pyrography tools and equipment

1. Fred Aldous Ltd.,
   P.O. Box 135,
   37 Lever Street,
   Manchester M60 1UX

2. The Leisurecrafts Centre,
   2–10 Jerdan Place,
   London, SW6 5PT

Wooden boxes, egg cups, shapes, etc.

1 and 2 above.

3. Hobby Horse,
   15 Langton Street,
   London, SW10

Woodwork tools

Most hardware stores and do-it-yourself shops. Also from

4. Dryad,
   Northgates,
   Leicester.

5. Flexitools,
   Albrighton,
   Wolverhampton.

Leather

4. above.

6. Rose (Fittings) Ltd.,
   337 City Road,
   London, EC1

7. A. L. Maugham & Co. Ltd.,
   5 Fazakerley Street,
   Liverpool, L3 9DN

Perspex acrylic sheets

8. Invicta Plastics Ltd.,
   Oadby,
   Leicester.

9. I. King,
   27 Houlton Street,
   St Pauls,
   Bristol 2

Ivory

To find a supplier in your own area don't forget that the yellow pages classified directory can be helpful.

10. F. Friedlein,
    718 Old Ford Road,
    London, E3

Bibliography

Woodwork

Practical Woodcarving and Gilding. William Wheeler and Charles H. Hayward. Evans Brothers Limited.

Modern Woodturning. Gordon Stokes. Evans Brothers Limited.

Colouring, Finishing and Painting Wood. Newell and Holtrop.

The Complete Book of Wood Finishing. Robert Scharf. Faber and Faber.

Design

Ideas for Decoration. Robert Seguin and Marthe Seguin-Fontes. Evans Brothers Limited.

A Treasury of Design for Artists and Craftsmen. Dover.

Pattern Design. Dover.